NERD
CULTURE

NERDING OUT ABOUT
DIY

VIRGINIA LOH-HAGAN

45th Parallel Press

Published in the United States of America by Cherry Lake Publishing Group
Ann Arbor, Michigan
www.cherrylakepublishing.com

Reading Adviser: Beth Walker Gambro, MS, Ed., Reading Consultant, Yorkville, IL
Book Designer: Joseph Hatch

Photo Credits: © Svitlana, Adobe Stock, cover, title page; © dekazigzag/Shutterstock, 4; © BongkarnGraphic/Shutterstock, 7; © FabrikaSimf/Shutterstock, 8; © Ladanifer/Shutterstock, 10; © Stokkete/Shutterstock, 12; © Nattapat.J/Shutterstock, 15; © Elnur/Shutterstock, 16; © Gorodenkoff/Shutterstock, 19; © Yuriy Golub/Shutterstock, 21; © TinoFotografie/Shutterstock, 22; © Frame Stock Footage/Shutterstock; © gpointstudio/Shutterstock, 26; © allensima/Shutterstock, 28; © FellowNeko/Shutterstock, 29

45th Parallel Press is an imprint of Cherry Lake Publishing Group.

Library of Congress Cataloging-in-Publication Data has been filed and is available at catalog.loc.gov

Cherry Lake Publishing Group would like to acknowledge the work of the Partnership for 21st Century Learning, a Network of Battelle for Kids. Please visit Battelle for Kids online for more information.

Note from publisher: Websites change regularly, and their future contents are outside of our control. Supervise children when conducting any recommended online searches for extended learning opportunities.

Printed in the United States of America

Dr. Virginia Loh-Hagan is an author and educator. She is currently the Director of the Asian Pacific Islander Desi American (APIDA) Center at San Diego State University and the Co-Executive Director of The Asian American Education Project. She lives in San Diego with her very tall husband and very naughty dogs.

TABLE OF CONTENTS

Some people are nerds about figuring things out for themselves. They create things and fix things.

LIVING THE NERDY LIFE

It's finally cool to be a nerd. Nerd culture is everywhere. It's in movies. It's on TV. It's in video games. It's in books. Everyone is talking about it. Everyone is watching it. Everyone is doing it. There's no escaping nerd culture.

Nerds and sports fans are alike. They have a lot in common. Instead of sports, nerds like nerdy things. Magic is nerdy. Science fiction is nerdy. Superheroes are nerdy. Nerds obsess over these interests. They're huge fans. They have a great love for a topic. They learn all they can. They spend hours on their hobbies. Hobbies are activities. Nerds hang with others who feel the same.

Nerds form **fandoms**. Fandoms are nerd networks. They're communities of fans. Nerds host online group chats. They host meetings. They host **conventions**. Conventions are large gatherings. They have speakers. They have workshops. They're also called **expos**. Tickets sell fast. Everyone wants to go. Nerd conventions are the place to be.

Nerd culture is on the rise. It's very popular. But it didn't used to be. Nerds used to be bullied. They were made fun of. They weren't seen as cool. They'd rather study than party. This made them seem odd. They were seen as different. Not anymore! Today, nerds rule!

Today, many people learn how to do things themselves through helpful videos.

DIY fans take an "I can do it" attitude.

CHAPTER 1

HANDS-ON CULTURE

DIY stands for do-it-yourself. People need things. Things break. They need to be fixed. This can be costly. Some people would rather make their own things. They'd rather fix things themselves. They don't want to pay **professionals**. Professionals are people with skills. They often charge a lot of money.

Nerd culture supports DIY thinking. Nerds create their own experiences. They like things in a certain way. They build their own things. They make toys. They make tools. They fix things. They make **mods**. This term is short for modifications. Modification means change. In gaming, players make mods. They make changes to games.

DIY fans join online groups. They have online sites. They make videos. They make their work public.

DIY fans want to be real. They want to be hands-on. They want to try new hobbies. They teach themselves. They try things out. They're open. They share their ideas. They share resources. They're **transparent**. They talk about their process. They make mistakes. They're not afraid to fail.

DIY supports the maker movement. Makers use STEAM skills. STEAM means science, technology, engineering, art, and math. Makers think about design. They solve problems. They create new devices. They tinker with existing devices.

Many DIY fans go to maker faires. These faires are conventions. They showcase makers' work. Makers can share their learning with others. They can sell their goods.

Men and women wrote letters to newspapers. They sought DIY advice for their homes.

CHAPTER 2

MAKING HISTORY

People have always had to build things. But things changed in the 1900s. More tech was invented. More people started businesses. People didn't have to do as many things. They relied on others. They relied on machines. They could easily buy things. They could pay people to do things.

Starting in the 1950s, there was a return to DIY thinking. DIY started with home projects. People wanted to improve their homes. They wanted to fix their houses. Today, there are many shows about home improvement.

At first, the goal of the DIY movement was to save money. The United States had just finished fighting in wars. There were limited resources.

ALPHA
Alpha refers to early models. They're first drafts. They're not ready to be used. They need to be tested.

DIT or DIWO
DIT means do-it-together. DIWO means do-it-with-others. These terms refer to teamwork. They refer to collaboration. Some projects need more than one person.

FAB LAB
Fab labs are fabrication laboratories. Fabrication means the action of making. Fab labs are tech workshops. They're spaces to make electronics. They have lots of tech tools.

ITERATE
Iterate means to update. Iterations mean different versions. As products get tested, they get better.

PROTOTYPES
Prototypes are early models. They're first examples of a design. They're ready for testing. These models are not complete. But they work. They're used for demonstrations. They're also called beta.

TURNKEY
Turnkey means ready to go. Turnkey products are complete. They can be used right away. They don't need to be fixed. They don't need much work.

Today, DIY is cool. It's not about saving money. In some cases, it's cheaper buying than making things. People like homemade things. They feel they're more real. DIY fans want to have one-of-a-kind products. They want to express their personalities. They want to make art. They also want to save the environment. They reduce. They recycle. They reuse. They feel a sense of accomplishment. They take pride in their work.

The media has made DIY culture popular. There are DIY magazines. There are DIY social media platforms. There are DIY small businesses. There are DIY videos. People can learn anything online. DIY fans can easily learn new skills. YouTube has millions of how-to videos.

IKEA is a furniture store. People buy supplies. They use the supplies to build furniture themselves. The IKEA effect promoted DIY culture.

People personalize computers to fit their needs.

CHAPTER 3

SHOWCASING SKILLS

Nerds like to **customize**. Customizing means to build or fix something to fit a person's tastes. There are different DIY examples. An example is building a custom computer.

Nerds use computers for many things. They're used to play games. They're used to write. They're used to engage in online activities. Some nerds want their own computers. They think about power. They think about storage. They think about features.

They build their own programs. They learn to **code**. They create instructions for a computer. Some DIY fans learn to **hack**. Hack means to break into computers.

NERD TO KNOW!

Ashley Basnight is a DIY influencer. Influencers are social media stars. They inspire others. Basnight is a computer engineer. She helps build planes. She works in Oklahoma. She wanted a kitchen table. She couldn't find the one she wanted. So she built her own. She taught herself. Three years later, she has her own business. Her business is called Handmade Haven. Today, Basnight is a woodworking expert. She works in her garage. She builds furniture. She designs homes. She makes closets and much more. She's been on TV shows. She said, "I enjoy being able to show people that you don't have to have a background in making or look the part in order to be creative and make beautiful things." She supports women. She supports people of color. She said, "People are still surprised when I say I build things. I want to show women we can do it. We're just as strong."

Some DIY tech fans build their own keyboards. Keyboards have letters and numbers. They're used to input information into computers. There are different types of keyboards.

Some nerds care about how keyboards look. They care about how keyboards feel. They care about how keyboards sound. They design their own. There are many decisions to make. People choose the size. They choose the colors. They choose the layout of the keys. They choose the keyboard case. They choose key functions. They choose **keycaps**. Keycaps are key covers. They're used for typing. Some keyboards can be fancy. They can light up.

Making your own keyboard requires soldering. Soldering joins things by melting metals.

DIY fans customize more than just tech. They also customize their clothes. Clothes become wearable art.

Nerds like to collect things. Many nerds collect sneakers. Customizing sneakers is trendy. Some shoe companies have custom shops. Buyers choose colors. They choose materials. They choose designs. Another trend is to draw on sneakers. Some people draw with markers or paints. Some add fabrics. Some sew on designs. Another way to customize is to rebuild sneakers. People take sneakers apart. Then they put them back together. But they use different materials.

Upcycle means to make new products with old products. DIY fans take old clothes. They sew on new designs. They create new pieces.

Personalization is the purpose of DIY! DIY nerds make unique things.

People can spend hours making costumes.

Role-playing is a big part of nerd culture. It's acting. People act like a character. They change their looks. They change their behaviors. They pretend. Nerds like to **cosplay**. Cosplay means costume play. It's performance art. DIY is part of cosplay. Many fans make their own costumes. They make their own props. They learn to sew. They learn to craft. They learn to apply makeup.

Cosplayers show off their costumes. They go to fan conventions. They go to parades. They go to parties. They dress up to play games. Nerds like to play role-playing games. They play in character.

Many DIY fans use **3D printers**. 3D printers are tools. They print objects. They print things in 3D. 3D means three-dimensional. 3D items are not flat. They have depth, width, and length. DIY fans input codes into a computer. The computer prints out the design. It does this by building layers of material together.

Jasper Tan is a DIY *Star Wars* fan. He's from Singapore. He makes *Star Wars* collectibles. He uses his 3D printer. He's made more than 100 items. His work is displayed all over his house.

There's an online group for fans of 3D printing. Fans share their work. They share tips.

3D printing is used in medicine. It may be used to make human organs in the future.

TOO NERDY!

Is there such a thing as too much DIY? One company is using the DIY mentality to figure out what to do with human poop. A person produces about 1 pound (.45 kilograms) of poop a day. Think about how many people live on Earth. That's a lot of poop. Poop can't be saved. It has to be discarded. It can be unsafe. It can spread sickness. Some scientists and engineers want to fix poop. They want to make poop useful. Sanivation is a company. It works with countries in Africa. It gives toilets to poor communities. It collects the toilets. It treats the human waste. Human poop has lignin. Lignin can be found in wood and bark. Sanivation heats the lignin. It combines this with other fibers. Examples are sawdust and old plants. The poop becomes a sticky mix. This mix is shaped. It's dried. It becomes briquettes. Briquettes are blocks. They're used for fuel. They're used to start fires.

DIY fans and makers are critical thinkers.

CHAPTER 4

RELEASE YOUR INNER NERD

You, too, can be a DIY nerd! Try one of these activities!

TAKE THINGS APART!

Many makers practice **reverse engineering**. They break things apart. They unbuild things. They study each part. They study how things are connected. They study how things are made. This process is especially important for tech tools. It lets makers improve products. It lets makers find weak spots.

Makers don't have to start from scratch. They can look at existing designs. They learn from others. They study previous knowledge. They make products look better. They make products work better. They make products more useful.

SIGN UP FOR CLASSES!

Many DIY fans and makers are self-taught. They don't have professional training. They learn by doing. They don't do it for a living. Making tends to be a hobby. It's something extra.

Not having experience can be scary. Don't let that stop you. If you want to make something, do it. Watch videos. Take classes. Practice. Learn from mistakes. Keep trying. Keep improving.

See if your school has **makerspaces**. Makerspaces are workspaces. They can be found inside schools or libraries. They're workshop spaces. They have tools. They have supplies. People can learn together.

There are many online courses. There are also in-person courses.

Etsy is a popular online market.

PARTICIPATE IN A LOCAL MARKET!

Make things. Think about selling them. Think about being a small business owner. Some cities may have policies. They may require permits. Follow the laws.

Research local markets. Rent a table or booth space. Make your table look nice. Make sure you have plenty of **stock**. Stock is what you are selling. Make sure to have signs. Promote yourself.

Many DIY fans and makers sell online. Think about online markets. Create a website. Create social media. Share your work with others. People of all ages can get their hands and minds moving and making.

NERDY TIPS!

TIP #1

SHOP FOR USED GOODS.
GO TO THRIFT STORES.
GO TO YARD SALES.
GO TO FLEA MARKETS.
PEOPLE GET RID OF
THEIR JUNK. MANY OF
THESE THINGS STILL WORK.
THEY CAN BE SAVED.
THEY CAN BE REUSED.

TIP #2

GET DUCT TAPE.
DUCT TAPE IS A GREAT DIY TOOL.
DUCT TAPE IS MADE OF CLOTH.
IT'S STICKY. IT COMES IN DIFFERENT
COLORS. IT HAS MANY USES.
IT CAN BE USED TO COVER HOLES.
IT CAN BE USED TO REPAIR THINGS.
IT CAN BE USED TO FOR CRAFTS.

TIP #3

MANY MAKERS HAVE THEIR OWN WORKSHOPS. CREATE YOUR OWN SPACE. STORE YOUR TOOLS THERE. WORK ON YOUR PROJECTS THERE. ORGANIZE YOUR THINGS. LABEL YOUR TOOLS. KEEP YOUR SPACE CLEAN AND TIDY.

TIP #4

PUT SAFETY FIRST. DON'T GET HURT. CALL A PROFESSIONAL IF NEEDED. ONLY USE TOOLS YOU KNOW HOW TO USE.

TIP #5

AVOID HOARDING. HOARDERS COLLECT AND KEEP A LOT OF THINGS. THEY DON'T THROW ANYTHING AWAY. THEY CAN'T GET RID OF THINGS. ONLY KEEP THINGS YOU CAN USE.

GLOSSARY

3D printers (THREE-dee PRIN-terz) machines that create three-dimensional objects layer-by-layer using a computer-created design

code (KOHD) to program a computer

conventions (kuhn-VEN-shuhnz) large meetings of fans who come together to talk about and to learn more about a shared interest

cosplay (KAHZ-play) the practice of dressing up as a character from a movie, book, or video game

customize (KUH-stuh-myez) to build, fit, or alter according to specific needs or tastes

expos (EK-spohz) large public exhibitions

fandoms (FAN-duhmz) communities of fans; combines "fanatic" and "kingdom"

hack (HAK) to use a computer to gain unauthorized access to data in a system

keycaps (KEE-kaps) small covers of plastic, metal, or other material placed over the key switch of a computer keyboard

makerspaces (MAY-ker-spay-sez) collaborative workspaces located in schools or libraries with tools and supplies

mods (MAHDZ) short for modifications, which are changes made for improvement

professionals (pruh-FESH-nuhlz) people who do a job requiring special training, education, and skills

reverse engineering (rih-VERS en-juh-NEER-ing) the act of dismantling an object to see how it works

role-playing (ROHL-play-ing) the act of pretending to be another character

stock (STAHK) what you are selling

transparent (trans-PAIR-uhnt) having clear and obvious thoughts, feelings, or motives that are easily perceived

upcycle (UHP-sye-kuhl) to reuse discarded objects or material to create a product of higher quality or value than the original

LEARN MORE

Corfee, Stephanie. *Craft Lab for Kids: 52 DIY Projects to Inspire, Excite, and Empower Kids to Create Useful, Beautiful Handmade Goods* Beverly, MA: Quarry Books, 2020.

Leigh, Helen. *The Crafty Kids Guide to DIY Electronics: 20 Fun Projects for Makers, Crafters, and Everyone in Between.* New York, NY: McGraw Hill, 2018.

Loh-Hagan, Virginia. *D.I.Y. Make It Happen* series. Ann Arbor, MI: 45th Parallel Press, 2016.

INDEX